CW01507547

Published In The United Kingdom By

Written and Illustrated
By
Jennifer Anne Sly

Dedicated to Derek
Norman Gray
[The Real Derek]

Derek woke up feeling
very excited.
The smell of Christmas was in the
air.

He jumped into his clothes
and ran downstairs
to see what Santa
had left for him.

Derek found his present with his
name on it and
quickly, tore the wrapping off and
opened up the
box.
Wow, it was a Cowboy suit!
All sorts of ideas popped into his
mind as he
climbed into his cowboy chaps and
waistcoat.

My, Derek felt grand as he gazed at himself in the mirror.

He waited until the Christmas holidays were over and it was the first day back at school again.

He got ready for school early.

Fully dressed in his Cowboy outfit, Derek made his way to the door practicing his moves on the way.

He felt excited.

But - Derek's mother was having none of that.
"Oh no! you cannot go to school dressed
like that." She said

"How are my friends going to see me now." Thought Derek crossly.

Derek thought carefully...

Suddenly he knew what to do.

He slowly snuck to the shed and hid his
cowboy outfit in there to pick up
just before he left for school." Ooh,
Naughty Derek!

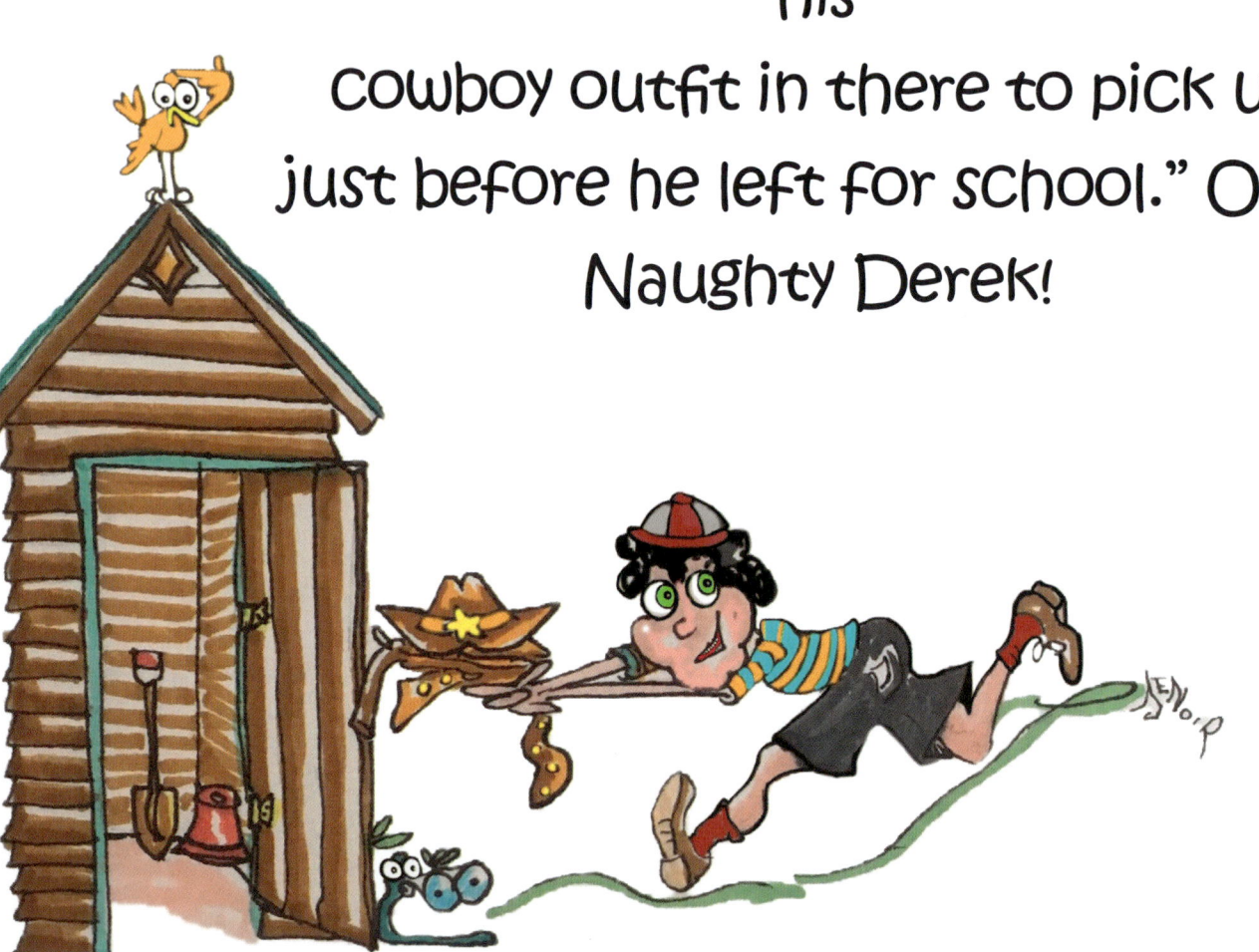

Then off he went to school, not forgetting
to pick up his bundle from the shed.

Derek was dying for breaktime so he could make his appearance in the playground.

In the meantime, Derek got down to the business of learning.

His teacher didn't know that she really was helping his creations.

The breaktime bell rang and Derek
dashed off to change.

Into the playground he burst!
pretending to ride a horse.
"Stick em' up!" He shouted.

Everybody stopped and gazed at
him in surprise.
Especially young Janet.
He put his moves into motion and
startled Rodney!

Derek had great fun, so much fun that when the bell rang for the end of breaktime, he forgot to take off his cowboy suit.

Derek strolled into class and took a seat.

The children thought he looked cool,
but Derek's teacher did not!

Derek had a long lip and was sent home
by his teacher.
He was laughed at by everyone except
Janet who was not impressed.

Derek took his long lip, and his
Cowboy suit home with him,
kicking cans along the way.

"How is a boy supposed to play, and
have fun." He thought crossly
On the way home.

Only his dog Trixi understood him.

Derek was not looking forward to
his haircut this afternoon.
Suddenly he sparked an idea!

...

What ever will Derek get up to now?

Be sure to find out what Derek did next!

...

Coming soon from the
'Don't Do What Derek Did'
Series:

'Derek's Bad Hair Day'

and

The Christmas Special:
'Dereks Ice-scapade'

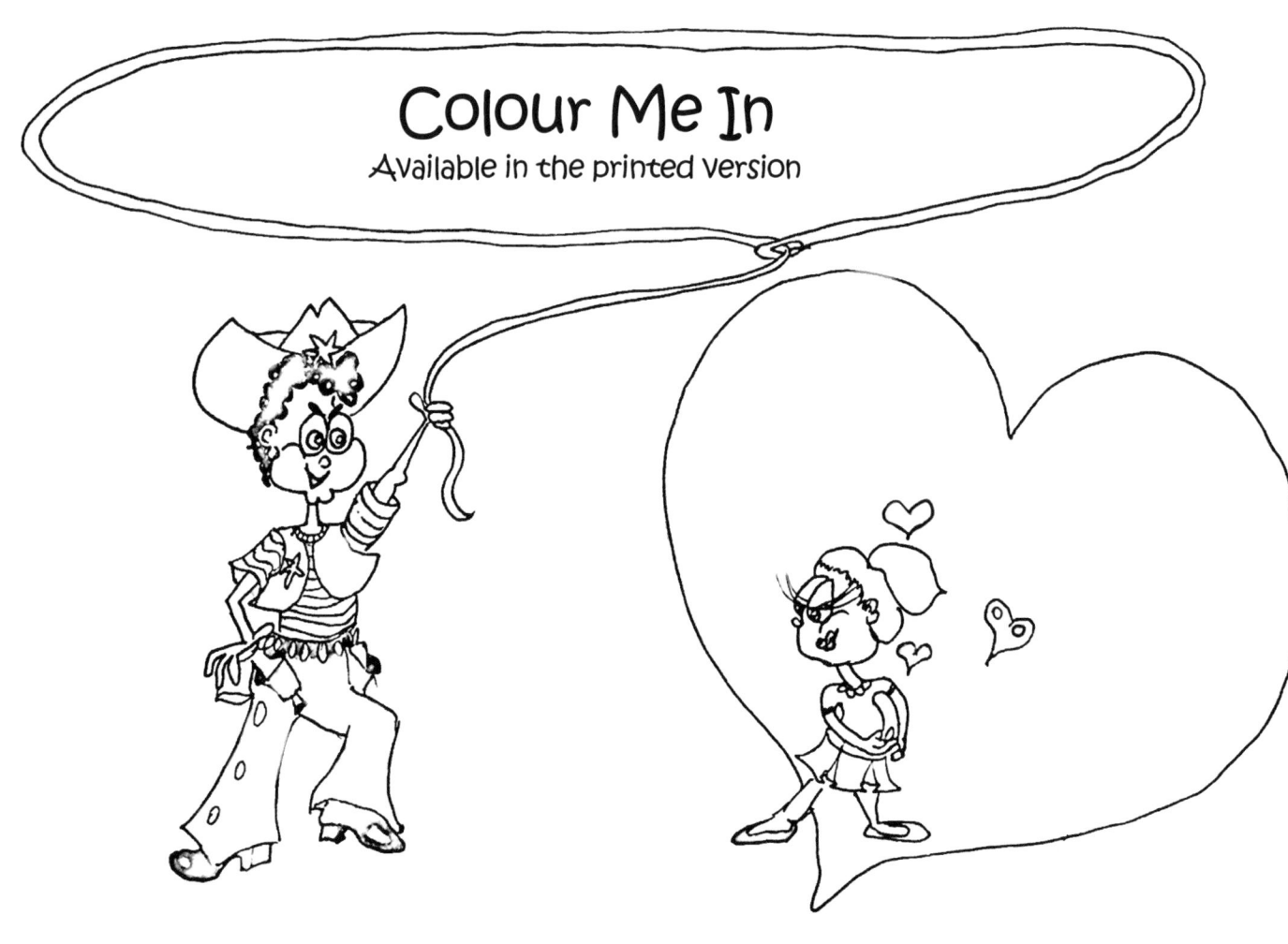

Colour me in

Printed in Poland
by Amazon Fulfillment
Poland Sp. z o.o., Wrocław

65787798R00016